The Antihero

Essential Literary Themes

by Jennifer Joline Anderson

Essential Library

An Imprint of Abdo Publishing | abdopublishing.com

abdopublishing.com

Published by Abdo Publishing, a division of ABDO, PO Box 398166, Minneapolis, Minnesota 55439. Copyright © 2016 by Abdo Consulting Group, Inc. International copyrights reserved in all countries. No part of this book may be reproduced in any form without written permission from the publisher. Essential Library™ is a trademark and logo of Abdo Publishing.

Printed in the United States of America, North Mankato, Minnesota
052015
092015

THIS BOOK CONTAINS RECYCLED MATERIALS

Cover Photo: Shutterstock Images
Interior Photos: Leemage/Corbis, 13; Théodore Chassériau, 15, 19; Everett Collection, 17, 23, 25, 36, 38, 45, 85; Photofest, 27, 89; Branwell Brontë, 33; Mary Evans/AIP/Ronald Grant/Everett Collection, 43, 50; Photo studio V. Lauffert /State Museum of History, Moscow/1872/Albumin Photo/Russia/Portrait (4266-18549) Superstock/Courtesy Everett Collection, 55; Franz Krüger, 57; Public Domain, 58; Vasily Perov, 65; Shutterstock Images, 71; Robert Kradin/AP Images, 77; Mary Evans/Argentina Sono Film S.A.C.I./Ronald Grant/Everett Collection, 79; Cinecom Pictures/Everett Collection, 82, 93, 96

Editor: Jenna Gleisner
Series Designer: Maggie Villaume

Library of Congress Control Number: 2015931117
Cataloging-in-Publication Data

Anderson, Jennifer Joline.
The antihero / Jennifer Joline Anderson.
   p. cm. -- (Essential literary themes)
Includes bibliographical references and index.
ISBN 978-1-62403-801-3
1. American literature--Themes, motives--Juvenile literature. 2. American literature--History and criticism--Juvenile literature. 3. Antiheroes in literature--Juvenile literature.   I. Title.
810--dc23
                                        2015931117

Contents

Chapter 1
Introduction to Themes in Literature   6

Chapter 2
An Overview of *Macbeth*   12

Chapter 3
Feminist Antihero   22

Chapter 4
An Overview of *Wuthering Heights*   32

Chapter 5
Romantic Antihero   42

Chapter 6
An Overview of
Notes from the Underground   54

Chapter 7
Alienated Antihero   64

Chapter 8
An Overview of *Native Son*   76

Chapter 9
Antihero as Social Protest   88

Analyze It!   100
Glossary   102
Characteristics and Classics 104
References   105

Additional Resources   106
Source Notes   108
Index   110
About the Author   112

1

INTRODUCTION TO

Themes in Literature

*D*o you find yourself drawn to the same types of stories? Are your favorite characters on a quest? Are they seeking revenge? Or are your favorite stories about love? Love, revenge, a quest—these are all examples of themes. Although each story is different, many stories focus on similar themes. You can expand your understanding of the books you read by recognizing the common themes within them.

What Is a Theme?

A theme is a concept or idea that shows up again and again in various works of art, literature, music, theater, film, and other endeavors throughout history. Some themes revolve around a story's plot. For example, a play about a young girl moving away from home and learning the ways of the world would be considered a coming of age story. But themes are not always so easily noticed. For example, a work might have allusions. Allusions are references, sometimes indirect, to other works or historical events. Themes might also relate to specific characters or subjects of a work. For example, many stories present heroes or villains. These common character types are often called archetypes.

How Do You Uncover a Theme?

Themes are presented in different ways in different works, so you may not always be aware of them. Many works have multiple themes. Uncover themes by asking yourself questions about the work. What is the main point or lesson of the story? What is the main conflict? What do the characters want? Where does the story take place? In many cases, themes may not be apparent until after a close study, or analysis, of the text.

What Is an Analysis?

Writing an analysis allows you to explore the themes in a work. In an analysis, you can consider themes in multiple ways. You can describe what themes are present in a work. You can compare one work to another to see how the presentation of a theme differs between the two forms. You can see how the use of a particular theme either supports or rejects society's norms. Rather than attempt to discover the author's purpose in creating a work, an analysis reveals what *you* see in the work.

Raising your awareness of themes through analysis allows you to dive deeper into the work itself. You may begin to see similarities between all creative works that you encounter. You may also improve your own writing by expanding your understanding of how stories use themes to engage readers.

Forming a Thesis

Form your questions about how a theme is presented in a work or multiple works and find answers within the work itself. Then you can create a thesis. The thesis is the key point in your analysis. It is your argument about the work. For example, if you want to argue that the theme of a book is love, your thesis could be worded as follows: Allison Becket's novel *On the Heartless Road* asserts that receiving love is critical to the human experience.

How to Make a Thesis Statement

In an analysis, a thesis statement typically appears at the end of the introductory paragraph. It is usually only one sentence long and states the author's main idea.

Providing Evidence

Once you have formed a thesis, you must provide evidence to support it. Evidence will usually take the form of examples and quotations from the work itself, often including dialogue from a character. You may wish to address what others have written about the work. Quotes from these individuals may help support your claim. If you find any quotes or examples that contradict your thesis, you will need to create an argument against them. For instance: Many critics claim the theme of love is secondary to that of revenge, as the main character, Carly, sabotages the lives of her loved ones throughout the novel. However, the novel's resolution proves that Carly's experience with love is the key to her humanity.

Concluding the Essay

After you have written several arguments and included evidence to support them, finish the essay with

How to Support a Thesis Statement

An analysis should include several arguments that support the thesis's claim. An argument is one or two sentences long and is supported by evidence from the work being discussed. Organize the arguments into paragraphs. These paragraphs make up the body of the analysis.

a conclusion. The conclusion restates the ideas from the thesis and summarizes some of the main points from the essay. The conclusion's final thought often considers additional implications for the essay or gives the reader something to ponder further.

How to Conclude an Essay

Begin your conclusion with a recap of the thesis and a brief summary of the most important or strongest arguments. Leave readers with a final thought that puts the essay in a larger context or considers its wider implications.

In This Book

In this book, you will read summaries of works, each followed by an analysis. Critical thinking sections will give you a chance to consider other theses and questions about the work. Did you agree with the author's analysis? What other questions are raised by the thesis and its arguments? You can also see other directions the author could have pursued to analyze the work. Then, in the Analyze It section in the final pages of this book, you will have an opportunity to create your own analysis paper.

The Antihero in Literature

The antihero is a main character in a literary work who is *not* heroic. Although most antiheroes are unlikeable or even despicable, they stop short of being outright villains because the reader sympathizes with them and roots for them. Also unlike traditional heroes and villains, antiheroes tend to be realistic, complex characters who are morally ambiguous—that is, neither all good nor all bad. Whereas heroes uphold the values of society, antiheroes often rebel against these values, acting in ways society believes they should not. They are often outsiders and rebels, alienated and outcast. For this reason, they are often figures of protest and social criticism and may be used to explore human psychology or challenge traditional notions of morality.

Look for the Guides

Throughout the chapters that analyze the works, thesis statements have been highlighted. The box next to the thesis helps explain what questions are being raised about the work. Supporting arguments have also been highlighted. The boxes next to the arguments help explain how these points support the thesis. The conclusions are also accompanied by explanatory boxes. Look for these guides throughout each analysis.

2

AN OVERVIEW OF
Macbeth

*W*illiam Shakespeare wrote the tragedy *Macbeth* around the year 1606. A tragedy is a play in which a hero of high status experiences a downfall, often caused by a tragic flaw such as pride or ambition. Shakespeare's tragedies are perhaps the most famous in the English language. The English playwright penned at least ten tragedies, including *Romeo and Juliet*, *Hamlet*, *Othello*, *King Lear*, and *Macbeth*.

Macbeth's tragic hero is Macbeth, a Scottish nobleman who murders the king of Scotland so he can take the king's place as ruler. Macbeth's wife, Lady Macbeth, is often seen as an antihero. She pushes her husband to commit the murder, making her another tragic hero.

While not the main character in *Macbeth*, Lady Macbeth plays a crucial role in the play's events.

Act 1: Strange Predictions

As the play opens, three witches are gathered in an open field. Nearby, Scottish soldiers are battling enemy forces. The witches hatch a plan to meet with Macbeth, one of the king's generals, when the battle is over. As the battle ends, King Duncan receives reports of Macbeth's heroism.

Macbeth leaves the battlefield with another general, Banquo. The witches greet the two men with mysterious prophesies. They hint Macbeth will gain a new title, Thane of Cawdor, and later become king of Scotland. They add that Banquo's descendants will also become kings. Macbeth is intrigued by these strange predictions of his future greatness, but Banquo warns him not to trust the witches, as they may have evil intentions.

Shortly afterward, Macbeth learns King Duncan has named him Thane of Cawdor as a reward for his heroism in battle. Macbeth is stunned to find the witches' first prediction has come true. He wonders whether the second prediction, that he will become king of Scotland, will also come true. Because King Duncan's son, Malcolm, is next in line for the throne, it seems to Macbeth he will have to kill both King Duncan and

Three witches appear to Macbeth and Banquo, prophesizing Macbeth's rise to power.

Prince Malcolm to fulfill the prediction. Thoughts of murder fill his mind, but he tries to hide them. In an aside to the audience, he says, "Stars, hide your fires: / Let not light see my black and deep desires."[1]

Back in their castle, Lady Macbeth reads a letter from her husband telling her about the witches' predictions. She is excited by the prospect of Macbeth becoming king and is prepared to murder the present King Duncan to make that happen. However, she worries Macbeth is too kind to do what needs to be done. She plans to talk him into it: "Hie thee hither," she addresses Macbeth in a soliloquy, "That I may pour my spirits in thine ear."[2] Lady Macbeth calls on evil spirits to "unsex" her, making her as cruel and unremorseful as a man so she can successfully carry out her evil plan.[3] When Macbeth returns with news that King Duncan will stay the night at their castle, Lady Macbeth tells her husband to look innocent and leave the rest to her; she will plan Duncan's murder.

Once the king arrives, Macbeth has second thoughts. In a soliloquy, he agonizes over their plan. Because Duncan is a virtuous king and Macbeth is bound by duty to protect him, Macbeth decides he cannot murder the king only to satisfy his own ambition. But Lady Macbeth again convinces him to go ahead with the plan. She scolds her husband for being cowardly and unmanly, claiming she would be ruthless enough to kill her own baby if she had sworn to do it. Macbeth worries they might fail, but Lady Macbeth responds with what she thinks is a foolproof plan. She will drug Duncan's attendants, causing them to fall asleep, allowing Macbeth to kill the unguarded king. Macbeth finally agrees, admiring Lady Macbeth's strength of spirit.

Macbeth feels instant guilt after committing murder.

Act 2: The King Is Murdered

Lady Macbeth serves the king's attendants drugged
wine. After they fall into a deep slumber, Macbeth
enters Duncan's bedroom and stabs the sleeping king.
When the deed is done, Macbeth is horrified. He
imagines he hears a voice crying out his guilt. Lady
Macbeth finishes the job for him by smearing the

sleeping servants' daggers and faces with blood, framing them for the murder. Returning from the scene of the crime, she finds Macbeth looking at his bloody hands with horror and scolds him again for being cowardly.

As Macbeth and Lady Macbeth hurry to wash the blood from their hands, they hear knocking at the castle gate. Two other noblemen, Macduff and Lennox, arrive at the castle. Entering the king's chamber to greet him, Macduff discovers the king's murdered body. Macbeth pretends to be shocked and furious. He storms into the bedroom and kills the king's attendants, pointing out they were covered in blood and thus must have been to blame for the murder. Lady Macbeth pretends to faint at the news and is carried away.

Banquo, Macduff, and Lennox appear to believe Macbeth's story, but the king's sons, Malcolm and Donalbain, suspect Macbeth. Malcolm and Donalbain flee the castle to avoid becoming Macbeth's next victims. Because the princes flee, suspicion falls on them for having killed Duncan, and Macbeth is declared king.

Act 3: The Truth Revealed

Macbeth holds a feast to celebrate his coronation. Recalling the witches' third prediction that Banquo's

Macbeth's guilt haunts him to the point of hallucination.

descendants will be kings, he hires men to kill Banquo
and his son Fleance on the day of the feast. The men
kill Banquo, but Fleance escapes. Macbeth thinks he
sees Banquo's ghost at the table during the feast. Guests
are shocked to see Macbeth talking to what looks like
an empty chair. Lady Macbeth covers up by claiming
Macbeth is suffering from a strange illness, but the scene
causes the other lords to suspect the truth. Lennox and
Macduff plan to join Duncan's sons. They also plan to
put together an army to dethrone Macbeth.

Act 4: False Courage

In act 4, Macbeth consults the witches. They repeat the prediction that Banquo's descendants will rule Scotland, but they mislead Macbeth into thinking he is invincible, predicting: "None of woman born / Shall harm Macbeth"[4] and "Macbeth shall never vanquished be until / Great Birnam wood to high Dunsinane Hill / Shall come against him."[5]

Armed with false courage, Macbeth becomes even more ruthless. Learning Macduff has sided against him, he orders the murder of Macduff's wife and children while Macduff is in England meeting with Malcolm. Macduff is devastated by the murder of his family and vows revenge.

Act 5: The Tragic End

In the final act, Lady Macbeth is left alone in the castle while Macbeth gathers his troops. Tormented by guilt over the murders, she begins walking in her sleep and washing her hands repeatedly, thinking she sees blood. "Out, damned spot! out, I say!" she yells.[6]

Macbeth returns with troops to defend the castle. His generals report Malcolm is preparing to attack, but Macbeth remains confident, trusting the witches' predictions that he will not be vanquished. As he waits, he hears a cry. Servants report Lady Macbeth has killed herself. Macbeth, hearing his queen is gone, despairs because of the meaninglessness of life. "Out, out, brief candle!" he says in a famous speech. "Life's but a walking shadow, a poor player / That struts and frets his hour upon the stage, / And then is heard no more. / It is a tale / Told by an idiot, full of sound and fury, / Signifying nothing."[7]

Meanwhile, Malcolm's men surround the castle, using branches from the trees of Birnam Forest as camouflage. Macbeth realizes the witches' prediction has come true: Birnam Wood has come to Dunsinane in the form of disguised troops. Still, he vows to fight bravely, taking heart in the witches' other prediction that he cannot be killed by any man born of a woman. As Macbeth faces off with Macduff, Macduff reveals he was "untimely ripped" from his mother's womb— meaning he was delivered by cesarean section and not born in the usual sense.[8] Macbeth finally realizes the witches have tricked him again, and he is doomed. Macduff kills Macbeth. In the final scene, Malcolm is hailed king of Scotland.

Feminist Antihero

*L*ady Macbeth is one of the most wicked characters in English literature. Shakespeare's audience likely saw her as a villainous temptress. Feminist critics, however, have a more sympathetic view of Lady Macbeth. They examine how women are represented in a work of literature, often describing how female characters reflect attitudes toward women at the time the work was written. Viewed from a feminist perspective, Lady Macbeth can be seen as a

Thesis Statement

The last sentence of the first paragraph is this essay's thesis statement. It reads: "Viewed from a feminist perspective, Lady Macbeth can be seen as a feminist antihero, rebelling against the submissive role of womanhood in a male-dominated society." This essay will focus on the characteristics of Lady Macbeth that make her an antihero.

Lady Macbeth proves herself an antihero through her wicked and greedy schemes.

feminist antihero, rebelling against the submissive role of womanhood in a male-dominated society.

Argument One

The first sentence after the thesis statement serves as the first argument: "As a strong, ambitious woman with a powerful influence over her husband, Lady Macbeth is far from the Renaissance ideal of womanhood." In this section, the author will support the thesis by explaining the ways in which Lady Macbeth controls her husband.

As a strong, ambitious woman with a powerful influence over her husband, Lady Macbeth is far from the Renaissance ideal of womanhood. Shakespeare's England was a patriarchal society. Women were expected to obey their husbands and fathers and fulfill their roles as loving and nurturing mothers. The qualities of courage and strength were associated with men, not women. But rather than look to her husband for guidance, Lady Macbeth seeks a leadership role in her marriage. After reading Macbeth's letter in act 1, Lady Macbeth laments that he is "too full of the milk of human kindness" to achieve his goal of becoming king.[1] "Hie thee hither," she calls to her husband in soliloquy, "that I may pour my spirits in thine ear / And chastise with the valor of my tongue / All that impedes thee from the golden round."[2]

Lady Macbeth holds control in her marriage, guiding Macbeth's actions both before and after the murder.

By declaring she will chastise, or scold, her husband, she indicates she has an equal role in their marriage, if not a dominant one. She is confident she can guide Macbeth to the "golden round," or crown, with her courage and strength of spirit.

Contrary to the stereotype of women as gentle-hearted ladies, Lady Macbeth's ruthless determination makes her appear stronger and more

Argument Two

The second argument states: "Contrary to the stereotype of women as gentle-hearted ladies, Lady Macbeth's ruthless determination makes her appear stronger and more masculine than her husband." Lady Macbeth takes power into her own hands, becoming her husband's equal.

masculine than her husband. Lady Macbeth acts as the leader throughout the first two acts of the play. She dictates the plan for King Duncan's murder and convinces a hesitant Macbeth to go through with it. When Macbeth is overcome with dread after killing the king, Lady Macbeth, unshaken, finishes the deed by planting the daggers and smearing the sleeping servants' faces with blood. Finding Macbeth staring in horror at the blood on his hands, she shows him her own bloody hands, scolding: "My hands are of your color; but I shame / To wear a heart so white."[3] As Macbeth's guilty conscience causes him to see visions and ghosts, he again seems less masculine than Lady Macbeth. She scolds him for acting as a superstitious old woman: "This is the very painting of your fear. . . . A woman's story at a winter fire, / Authorized by her grandma."[4]

Argument Three

The final argument of the essay focuses on Shakespeare's portrayal of Lady Macbeth as an antihero: "By showing Lady Macbeth's remorse and eventual downfall at the end of the play, Shakespeare actually reveals her humanity."

By showing Lady Macbeth's remorse and eventual downfall at the end of the play, Shakespeare actually reveals her humanity. Some may see Lady Macbeth's downfall as Shakespeare's way of putting

Macbeth's bravery pales in comparison to Lady Macbeth's.

a wicked woman in her place and reaffirming to his audience that, after all, women are too weak to do the deeds men do. Indeed, Shakespeare's audience may have been satisfied to see the villainous queen punished for her evil deeds. However, that may not be the message Shakespeare intended.

In her grief and remorse, Lady Macbeth appears less like a stock villain or wicked temptress and more like a complex and deeply flawed tragic hero who has overstepped the boundaries of morality and paid the price. Some readers may even see her as a feminist antihero who challenged the patriarchy, daring to do what her society thought a lady could never do.

Conclusion

The last paragraph of this essay serves as the conclusion. It points out there are several ways to interpret Shakespeare's depiction of Lady Macbeth, but that she is arguably a feminist antihero.

Thinking Critically

Now it's your turn to assess the essay. Consider these questions:

1. After reading the essay, do you believe Lady Macbeth rebels against a male-dominated society? Why or why not?

2. Review the supporting arguments in the essay. Which argument is most convincing, and why? Which, if any, do you find unconvincing? What evidence could be added to strengthen the supporting arguments?

3. Do you agree Lady Macbeth is an antihero? Why or why not?

Other Approaches

In the essay you have just read, the author uses feminist criticism to analyze the character of Lady Macbeth. However, this is only one way to approach the theme of the antihero in *Macbeth*. Other ways to look at *Macbeth* could include historical criticism or archetypal criticism.

Witchcraft in *Macbeth*

Historical criticism attempts to examine a work of literature with reference to its historical context. Shakespeare wrote *Macbeth* shortly after King James I ascended the throne of England. King James was a Christian and a strong believer in the supernatural. During his reign, he ordered many women executed for witchcraft. A possible thesis statement that examines the play through this angle might be: Shakespeare intentionally characterized Macbeth as a tragic hero who is murdered after following the advice of witches to reflect on common religious beliefs of the time.

The Tragic Hero

Archetypal criticism examines elements of a literary work with respect to universal archetypes, or commonly recurring characters or types. The archetype of the tragic hero was first described by the ancient Greek philosopher Aristotle, who examined how this character was presented in classical Greek tragedies such as *Antigone* and *Medea*. According to Aristotle, the hero of a tragedy is a character of high status doomed by a fatal flaw. This flaw, typically pride or ambition, leads to the character's downfall. Both Macbeth and Lady Macbeth may be considered tragic heroes. A possible thesis statement that analyzes the play using archetypal criticism might be: As flawed tragic heroes led astray by pride and ambition, Macbeth and Lady Macbeth more closely resemble antiheroes than conventional heroes or villains.

AN OVERVIEW OF
Wuthering Heights

*W*uthering Heights is the first and only novel published by English writer Emily Brontë (1818–1848), sister of novelists Charlotte and Anne Brontë. It tells the tragic tale of two lovers, Cathy and Heathcliff, whose doomed love curses them and their descendants to a hellish misery.

Brontë's novel, with its atmosphere of gloom, mystery, and horror, shows the influence of Gothic fiction. Gothic novels were popular during the Romantic period of European literature, which spanned from approximately the late 1700s to the mid-1800s. Gothic novels are typically set in forbidding castles. They feature sinister villains who threaten young and innocent

Sisters Anne, *left*, Emily, *center*, and Charlotte, *right*, were all
novelists during the romantic period.

beauties, who then need saving by a virtuous and kind hero. But in *Wuthering Heights*, Brontë creates a twist on the traditional Gothic tale.

The character of Heathcliff is a combination of the villain and the hero, otherwise known as a Byronic hero. George Gordon, Lord Byron, was a leading poet of the romantic movement. The poet's famous dark good looks and roguish personality bled onto the page as Byron modeled the womanizing heroes of his romantic poetry after himself. Other writers began imitating him, and this so-called Byronic hero became a rebel and outcast. Not entirely heroic, the Byronic hero often appears villainous and cruel. Instead of being gentlemanly, Byronic heroes are wild, untamed, and uncivilized, with close ties to the natural world. The rebellious Byronic hero, which captures the spirit of the romantic era, describes Brontë's character Heathcliff.

Unwelcoming Host

Wuthering Heights is told in flashback by a man named Mr. Lockwood, a tenant of Heathcliff's. As the story begins, Lockwood has just moved into Heathcliff's pleasant country manor called Thrushcross Grange. Heathcliff is dark-skinned and handsome and dresses well, yet he is gruff and rude. His house, a dilapidated mansion called Wuthering Heights, sits on the edge of a vast moor with fiercely wuthering winds and neighbors Thrushcross Grange. The household appears just as wild. Heathcliff keeps a pack of dogs and only one servant, an unfriendly old man, in the house. When Lockwood is ready to leave after a visit, he is prevented by a blizzard. Heathcliff at first refuses to give him a place to sleep or a guide to lead him home. At last, Lockwood is allowed to sleep in an unused bedroom with no fire in the hearth.

Ghost at the Window

Unbeknownst to him, Lockwood is sleeping in the bedroom formerly occupied by Catherine Earnshaw, who grew up with Heathcliff at Wuthering Heights. Lockwood notices the names Catherine Earnshaw, Catherine Heathcliff, and Catherine Linton scratched into the paint on the windowsill. Before falling asleep, he peruses some old books in the room. One of them is labeled with the name Catherine Earnshaw along with a date from 25 years earlier. Lockwood discovers some of the blank pages in the books contain diary entries written by Catherine as a child. In one entry, Catherine

Heathcliff's character is a well-dressed and successful, yet rude and rough host.

describes a terrible Sunday in which she and Heathcliff are scolded and beaten for playing on the Sabbath. After scampering out of the house onto the moors, they are beaten even more harshly by her brother Hindley, who then forbids Heathcliff to sit or eat with the family or play with Catherine anymore.

Lockwood falls asleep while reading. In the middle of the night, he is awakened by a branch tapping on the window. He falls back to sleep and has a nightmare. In the dream, he opens the window and attempts to break off the branch, but the ghost of a little girl seizes his arm with an icy grip. She sobs to be let into the room, saying she is Catherine Linton and has lost her way on the moor. Lockwood wakes, screaming. Lockwood's screams awaken Heathcliff, who ejects him from the room. To Lockwood's amazement, Heathcliff then opens the window and calls out to the ghost, sobbing, "Come in! come in! Cathy, do come."[1] The next day, Heathcliff treats his daughter-in-law, also named Cathy, with cruelty, verbally abusing her and threatening to beat her. Lockwood is shocked and mystified.

An Orphaned Boy

Once he returns to Thrushcross Grange, Lockwood asks the housekeeper, Ellen "Nelly" Dean, about Heathcliff's behavior. She explains the history behind Wuthering Heights and its mysterious master, Heathcliff. As Nelly narrates, the action flashes back 30 years, when Cathy's father, Mr. Earnshaw, owns Wuthering Heights. Mr. Earnshaw returns from a visit to Liverpool, England, with an orphaned boy he found on the streets. He names the boy Heathcliff and raises him alongside his own children, Hindley and Catherine (Cathy). Heathcliff and Cathy become best friends. Hindley, however, is jealous

The orphaned Heathcliff, *center,* is brought into the Earnshaw home.

of his father's affection for the boy and relentlessly bullies Heathcliff. Heathcliff grows sullen and cold, vowing revenge on Hindley someday.

After Mr. Earnshaw's death, Hindley takes over as master and treats Heathcliff as a servant. Heathcliff and Cathy remain friends. One day, while running across the moors, they spy on their neighbors, the Lintons, who own the neighboring estate, Thrushcross Grange. Peering through the window, they see the Linton children, Edgar and Isabella, fighting with each other. As Heathcliff and Cathy laugh at these spoiled rich kids, the Lintons's dog attacks them, biting Cathy's ankle and injuring it severely. The Lintons take Cathy into their home until she can recover from the wounds. Heathcliff, however, is sent away amid insults calling him "a wicked boy" with the appearance of a gypsy fortuneteller or "Spanish castaway."[2] When Cathy returns, she is dressed as a fine lady and has manners picked up from her time with the Lintons. She laughs at Heathcliff for having dirty hands. Heathcliff grows jealous as Cathy continues to visit the Lintons and spend more time with them than she does with him.

One day after Edgar Linton has visited, Cathy confesses to Nelly that Edgar has asked her to marry him and she plans to accept. She admits to Nelly she really loves Heathcliff, but because her brother Hindley has brought him so low, it would degrade her to marry him. Heathcliff, eavesdropping from the kitchen, overhears her and runs away from Wuthering Heights in rage and humiliation. Cathy, who truly loves Heathcliff, is distraught and falls into a fever when she learns he is gone. She eventually recovers and marries Edgar.

Heathcliff's Return

Heathcliff returns several years later a wealthy man. Cathy is overjoyed to see him and hopes to renew their friendship. Instead, Heathcliff, furious she has married Edgar, plans revenge. He takes control of Wuthering

Heights from Hindley, now an alcoholic widower with gambling debts, and raises Hindley's son Hareton to be a rough, uneducated boor. Despite Cathy's protests, Heathcliff begins courting Edgar's sister, Isabella Linton, whom he actually despises. When Edgar learns of Heathcliff's interest in Isabella, he forbids Heathcliff to visit. Cathy, angry with both Heathcliff and Edgar, shuts herself in her bedroom and refuses to eat. She grows weaker and begins raving and experiencing visions, imagining she is once again a child with Heathcliff at Wuthering Heights.

Meanwhile, Heathcliff elopes with Isabella and then abuses her cruelly. When Nelly visits them at Thrushcross Grange, Heathcliff mocks Isabella for having been so silly as to think he was some sort of romantic hero. The abused Isabella calls him a monster and runs away from Heathcliff.

Heathcliff's cruelty torments Cathy, who dies of heartache shortly after giving birth to a daughter, Catherine. Heathcliff embraces Cathy on her deathbed, and the two passionately profess they have always loved each other. When she dies, Heathcliff howls, "Catherine Earnshaw, may you not rest, as long as I am living! You said I killed you—haunt me then!"[3]

Heathcliff's Revenge Continues

Some years later, Heathcliff's estranged wife, Isabella, dies, leaving their sickly son, Linton Heathcliff, in his care. Heathcliff begins a new evil plan. Through lies and manipulation, he encourages Cathy's daughter, Catherine, to fall in love with his son. Heathcliff locks Catherine in the house during a visit and holds her captive until she agrees to marry Linton. Linton dies shortly afterward of tuberculosis, and Catherine's father, Edgar, also dies—leaving Heathcliff in possession of Thrushcross Grange and guardian of Catherine. When Lockwood encounters them, Heathcliff's revenge seems complete. But far from satisfied, he still pines for Cathy. Ghoulishly, Heathcliff even bribes the sexton to dig up Cathy's grave so he can see her in the coffin, and he wanders the moors in search of her ghost. At last, he dies in his room with the window wide open to the moor where he believes Cathy has been roaming. He is soaked through with a freezing rain. On his face is a "life-like gaze of exultation," suggesting he has been reunited with Cathy at last.[4]

5

Romantic Antihero

$\mathcal{E}$ mily Brontë's novel, *Wuthering Heights*, the story of doomed lovers Cathy and Heathcliff, scandalized readers with its dark and disturbing themes and imagery when the book was published in 1847. Today, Brontë's novel is a classic of English literature. Readers who expect a traditional love story, however, will still be shocked by *Wuthering Heights*. A reader-response analysis of *Wuthering Heights* explores how the book continues to alternately fascinate and repulse readers through the mysterious character of Heathcliff. Reader-response criticism seeks to examine how readers respond to all or part of a literary work as they read. Heathcliff's unknown origins, exotic looks, and undying love for Cathy lead readers to see him as a brooding romantic

Heathcliff, the mysterious main character of *Wuthering Heights*, becomes the novel's antihero.

Thesis Statement

The thesis of the essay appears at the end of the first paragraph: "Emily Brontë defies readers' expectations for a conventional romance through her portrayal of Heathcliff as a dark and devilish antihero." This essay will highlight the ways in which Brontë illustrates the many ways to interpret Heathcliff's character.

Argument One

The first argument states: "Despite Heathcliff's forbidding appearance, readers are encouraged to see him as a romantic hero whose gruff exterior conceals a noble and sensitive heart." The author will explain how Heathcliff's appearance and personality traits cause readers to view him as a romantic or Byronic hero, or antihero.

hero. Yet in his vengeful and destructive behavior, he resembles a Gothic villain. The reader, with other characters in the novel, is continually forced to question Heathcliff's true nature. Is he a hero or a villain? Emily Brontë defies readers' expectations for a conventional romance through her portrayal of Heathcliff as a dark and devilish antihero.

Despite Heathcliff's forbidding appearance, readers are encouraged to see him as a romantic hero whose gruff exterior conceals a noble and sensitive heart. From the first lines of the book, Heathcliff is portrayed as a brutish, unpleasant

Heathcliff's features are repeatedly described as dark and villainous.

man. On meeting Lockwood, Heathcliff's "black eyes withdraw . . . suspiciously under their brows."[1] When he speaks, he growls. Lockwood finds him reserved. Heathcliff shows no courtesy to his guest and little concern when Lockwood is nearly attacked by his dogs. Heathcliff's malevolent nature is evident in his physical appearance, especially his eyes, the proverbial windows to the soul. Nelly describes his eyes as "black fiends" that glint under his half-closed lids "like devil's spies."[2] She says his "eyes full of black fire" hint at a "half-civilized ferocity" lurking underneath.[3]

But alongside these dark descriptions, readers are also introduced to a handsome and sensible character. Lockwood describes him as "a dark-skinned gipsy in aspect, in dress and manners a gentleman" and notes his "erect and handsome figure."[4] He appears surly, but Lockwood concludes approvingly that Heathcliff merely dislikes showing his emotions. Heathcliff's unmannerly behavior is shocking, especially as he curses his daughter-in-law and shows no concern for Lockwood's safety in the blizzard. But when Heathcliff cries out to what he thinks is the ghost of Cathy at the window, readers may be ready to excuse his surly behavior and continue to see him as a tortured romantic hero who is, at heart, a good man.

Heathcliff's past evokes sympathy and notions of heroism, but when he returns after seeking his fortune, readers find he has become a villain. A common characteristic of the

Argument Two

In the second argument, the author offers evidence that readers are led to think Heathcliff is vengeful rather than heroic: "Heathcliff's past evokes sympathy and notions of heroism, but when he returns after seeking his fortune, readers find he has become a villain."

romantic hero is his or her mysterious parentage. The hero may lead a life of poverty and obscurity, suffering mistreatment only to be revealed later as having been of noble birth. Heathcliff is an orphan boy, taken in by a kind gentleman, Earnshaw, who raises him as his own son. When Earnshaw dies, Heathcliff, Cinderella-like, is treated as a servant by Hindley. Yet even when Heathcliff is forced into this servant role, his exotic looks and mysterious past cause Nelly to imagine him as "a prince in disguise."[5] She tells Heathcliff encouragingly, "Who knows but your father was Emperor of China, and your mother an Indian queen."[6] Nelly's words encourage readers to expect Heathcliff will turn out to be some sort of noble, prince-like figure later in the story. Heathcliff's childhood relationship with Cathy reminds readers of a romance similar to Shakespeare's *Romeo and Juliet* in which the hero and heroine are torn apart by family and circumstance. Readers empathize with Heathcliff as he runs away from Wuthering Heights, heartbroken over Cathy's rejection, and hope he will be reunited with Cathy somehow or find a woman kinder than her who can appreciate him.

But similar to a typical villain, when he returns, Heathcliff takes away Wuthering Heights from its rightful owner, ripping away the rights of the true heir to the estate. His actions are so cruel they cannot be explained as the actions of a tortured romantic hero. Heathcliff beats his wife and shows himself incapable of loving even his own son, manipulating Linton into marriage. Young Catherine believes him to be a kind uncle until he kidnaps her as part of the plot. She begs to be returned to her dying father: "Mr. Heathcliff, you're a cruel man, but you're not a fiend; and you won't, from *mere* malice, destroy irrevocably all my happiness."[7] The reader expects at some point Heathcliff's heart will soften and he will repent. But Heathcliff is relentlessly malicious. He relishes the pain he causes others, bragging "the more the worms writhe, the more I yearn to crush out their entrails!"[8]

Brontë helps form a reader's response to Heathcliff through his relationships with women and the character Cathy. When Isabella offers Heathcliff her love, he returns it with cruelty, mocking her for having pictured him as "a hero of romance" who would provide "chivalrous devotion."[9] This quote is key to understanding Heathcliff. As noted by writer and critic Joyce Carol Oates, Heathcliff's mockery is directed at readers as well. By mocking him, readers are reminded of their expectations of Heathcliff and realize he is most certainly not a typical hero. Oates claims, "Brontë's wit in this passage is supreme, for she allows her 'hero' to define himself in opposition to a gothic-romantic stereotype she suspects her readers . . . cherish."[10]

Cathy is right to warn readers about romanticizing Heathcliff: "Pray, don't imagine that he conceals depths of benevolence and affection beneath a stern exterior! He's not a rough diamond—a pearl-containing oyster of a rustic: he's a fierce, pitiless, wolfish man."[11] Love to Heathcliff is wild and untamed, a force of nature. His love for Cathy is devouring, obsessive, and selfish, leading readers to view him more as an antihero.

In *Wuthering Heights,* Brontë intentionally shocks readers who expect a conventional romance novel. Ultimately, Heathcliff emerges as neither a hero nor a villain, but a morally complex antihero. Heathcliff dies with a wicked grin on his face, convinced he has, in

Throughout the novel, readers hope for a love connection between Heathcliff and Cathy.

Conclusion

This final paragraph is the conclusion of the critique. It summarizes the author's arguments and partially restates the original thesis, which has now been argued and supported with evidence.

death, been reunited with his Cathy—a happy ending of sorts. By skillfully reversing the typical happy ending, Brontë again defies readers' expectations of a traditional happily ever after romance.

Thinking Critically

Now it's your turn to assess the critique. Consider these questions:

1. After reading the essay, do you think the author did a good job of proving the thesis? Why or why not?

2. What was the most interesting argument made in this essay? What was the strongest one? What was the weakest? Were the points backed up with examples from the novel? Did the argument support the thesis?

3. Read the novel for yourself. Do you agree Heathcliff is neither a hero nor a villain? What do you believe about him? Is he fascinating, or repulsive, or both?

Other Approaches

The essay you have just read uses reader-response criticism to analyze *Wuthering Heights*, discussing the ways readers respond to the antiheroic character of Heathcliff. However, this is only one way to approach the theme of the antihero in *Wuthering Heights*. Below are two examples of other ways to approach this topic.

Cathy as Feminist Antihero

Viewed from a feminist perspective, can Cathy appear to be an antihero as well as Heathcliff? A thesis exploring this idea might be: The young Catherine Earnshaw—a wild, impetuous, impolite young woman—appears as a defiant antihero until her marriage to Edgar forces her to conform to the expectations of English society.

Comparing the Book with the Hollywood Version

This essay describes Heathcliff's character as portrayed in Emily Brontë's novel. Another essay might also analyze film interpretations of the novel, such as the 1939 classic starring Laurence Olivier and Merle Oberon. Is Heathcliff's character portrayed differently in the film version than in the novel? If so, how? A possible thesis statement that compares the book and a film adaptation might be: Hollywood movies tend to romanticize the character of Heathcliff, portraying him more sympathetically than he actually appears in Brontë's novel.

AN OVERVIEW OF
Notes from the Underground

*R*ussian author Fyodor Dostoyevsky (1821–1881) is considered one of the greatest writers of world literature. His writing shows a mature sense of human psychology and emphasizes the importance of free will and individuality.

Dostoyevsky came of age in Russia during a time of great philosophical activity and political unrest. Russian society was extremely unequal in the 1800s. Wealthy landowners lived off the labor of a poor and oppressed lower class. Many Russian thinkers called for a revolution that would end the rule of the Russian tsars and put in place a socialist government based on the ideas of German philosopher Karl Marx. As

In addition to *Notes from the Underground* (1864), Dostoyevsky is famed for his novel *Crime and Punishment* (1866).

a young man, Dostoyevsky became involved with a group of socialist thinkers who opposed the rule of the Russian ruler Tsar Nicholas I. In 1849, Dostoyevsky was arrested for treason and threatened with execution by firing squad before being imprisoned in a labor camp in Siberia.

After his imprisonment, Dostoyevsky was a changed man. He still favored social reform, but he no longer believed in socialist revolution. This put him at odds with radical Russian intellectuals of the 1860s. These socialist radicals, or nihilists, sought to sweep away traditional Russian morals and values, including religion, in favor of a brand-new society based on science and reason. They believed educating people about the right way to think could completely remove social problems and create an ideal society, a socialist utopia. The ideas of these thinkers led to a communist revolution in Russia in 1917.

Notes from the Underground is Dostoyevsky's rejection of the nihilists' idealistic vision. The novel is very unconventional. Half philosophical ramblings, half story, it is actually a brilliant parody that mocks nihilist thinking, while warning of the dangers this type of thinking poses to people's freedom. The nameless

Dostoyevsky opposed the rule of Tsar Nicholas I, *above*, resulting in Dostoyevsky's imprisonment in the mid-1800s.

protagonist, often called the Underground Man, is considered one of literature's first true antiheroes.

The Underground Man Speaks

Notes from the Underground is narrated by a 40-year-old retired government clerk in Saint Petersburg, Russia. He claims to be speaking from the "Underground," having withdrawn himself from society. In part 1, "Underground," he addresses his audience and gives a satirically humorous description of himself and his beliefs.

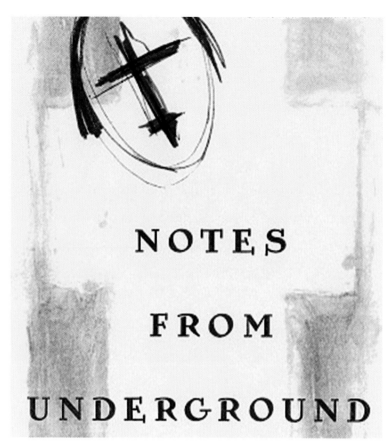

NOTES

FROM

UNDERGROUND

Throughout *Notes from the Underground*, the Underground Man continuously describes his pessimistic views of human nature.

The Underground Man introduces himself as a sick, wicked, and unattractive man. He confesses he has never managed to become anything in life, describing himself as "neither wicked nor good, neither a scoundrel nor an honest man, neither a hero nor an insect."[1] As an intelligent man, he has high ideals, but these principles only make him even more ashamed of his low and miserable state. Strangely, though, he takes pleasure in his misery and is resigned to it. He believes all conscious men suffer from a lack of energy to move forward; only foolish and narrow-minded people can accomplish anything because they are incapable of thinking too deeply.

The Underground Man describes his cynical view of human nature. In his view, humans are stubborn, irrational, unpredictable, and totally ungrateful. Faced with the hopelessness of getting the world to live up to his idealistic dreams, the Underground Man has decided to give up and retreat Underground.

Standoff on the Street

In part 2, "Apropos of the Wet Snow," the Underground Man tells three anecdotes from his younger life, when he was 24 years old and still attempting to live according to his lofty ideals. His life is "gloomy, disorderly, and solitary to the point of savagery."[2] People at work think he is odd. He hates himself and everyone else. He feels completely alienated, tormented by the thought that "no one else was like me, and I was like no one else. 'I am one, and they are *all.*'"[3] He is also prone to romantic ideas and longs for the types of adventures he has read about in books.

In search of such an adventure, he enters a tavern hoping to get into a brawl. As he stands watching a billiards game, a much taller soldier picks him up by the shoulders and moves him out of the way without even looking at him. Humiliated, the Underground Man obsesses for years over how to get his dignity back. He cannot challenge the soldier to a duel or he would be laughed at; and besides, he is far too cowardly. He writes a caricature ridiculing the soldier but cannot get it published. He writes a letter asking for an apology but never mails it. Finally, he decides on a subtle form of revenge: he will meet the soldier on the street and force him to move aside. He wants to look his best, so he borrows money for an expensive fur collar. After several failures, he finally manages to get in the soldier's path. The soldier bumps into him and keeps on walking, but the Underground Man exults in his victory, having stood up to the soldier and not moved aside for him.

Humiliated at the Class Party

In the second anecdote, the narrator joins his former classmates Simonov, Ferfichkin, and Trudolyubov, who are planning a party for another classmate, Zverkov, a successful army officer. The Underground Man does not have money and his clothes are shabby and worn, but he is determined to impress his former classmates at the party. While in school, his classmates had been petty and superficial; all they cared about was success. They all admired the rich and handsome Zverkov, even though he was vulgar and unintelligent. The narrator, on the other hand, who considers himself highly intelligent, was an outcast at school, mocked for his romantic ideas. Now, he fantasizes about becoming some sort of triumphant hero in their eyes.

The narrator arrives at the restaurant, having borrowed money to pay his share. His friends have not bothered to tell him the party was postponed from five o'clock until six o'clock in the evening, so he waits an hour, fuming. Zverkov arrives and greets the narrator with a superior attitude. He asks about the narrator's salary and comments it is quite low, adding that the narrator looks thin. After this conversation, everyone ignores the narrator and gathers around Zverkov, laughing at his stories. Humiliated, the narrator proceeds to get drunk and gives a speech insulting Zverkov: "I hate phrases, and phrase-mongers, and tight-fitting waists . . . gallantry and gallantizers," he rails, adding he loves "truth, sincerity, and honesty," "thought," and "true friendship."[4] The others laugh at him. They all go to visit a brothel and leave him behind.

Reforming a Prostitute

The Underground Man rushes to catch up to his friends, desperate to recover his lost pride. At the brothel, he is put in a room with a young prostitute named Liza. He begins lecturing her about her sorry state, encouraging her to become an honest woman. He paints a beautiful, idealistic picture of married love and motherhood. Although he feels he has made a beautiful argument, she observes he is talking like something out of a book. Angry, the narrator begins berating her and degrading her on more cruel terms, warning that if she continues her life as a prostitute, she will die alone and unloved. Finally she breaks down and cries, revealing her family has sold her into the life of a prostitute and she actually wants to get out. The narrator gives her his address and asks her to come to him.

The next morning, the narrator feels ashamed of his behavior at the party and attempts to recover his dignity with a carefully worded letter of apology to Simonov. He begins to despair over what will happen if Liza actually comes to see him. Then he fantasizes he will develop and educate her and they will fall in love. He is distracted from his fantasies by a power struggle with his servant, Apollon. He thinks Apollon is too haughty and wants to humiliate him by withholding the man's wages, forcing him to beg for the money, but Apollon refuses to beg, enraging him. The narrator is screaming wildly at Apollon when Liza comes to the door. The narrator is completely embarrassed to be found in a ragged bathrobe, screaming at his servant. He sobs and then strikes out at Liza, blaming her for humiliating him. To his surprise, she shows him love and understanding instead of scorn, and they make love.

Although Liza has shown him kindness and love, the Underground Man realizes he cannot love her back. Despite all his romantic words, he has never learned what love really is. All he can do is hate. Wanting to hurt her, he tells her to leave and shoves money into her hand. She throws it on the table and goes out. He rushes out to find her, but she is gone. He then tries consoling himself, telling himself this is better and lofty suffering is better than cheap happiness. Looking back years later, he realizes he was wrong. By clinging to false ideals and railing against moral corruption, he has denied himself an opportunity for real love.

Alienated Antihero

*A*t the end of part 1 of Dostoyevsky's *Notes from the Underground*, the Underground Man imagines his readers are shaking their heads at the "logical tangle" he has created, as well as the lies and inconsistencies in his writing.[1] But although his words appear to ramble, they actually form a series of arguments against the radical principles of socialism and utilitarianism, which Dostoyevsky believed were based on a simplistic view of human nature.

Socialists hoped to create a society in which all people held equal power and followed the philosophy of utilitarianism—that is, the belief that moral decisions should be made on the basis of the greater good for the greater number of people. However, the Underground

Dostoyevsky purposely created the Underground Man as an antihero.

Thesis Statement

The thesis statement comes at the end of the first paragraph: "Through the defiantly antiheroic character of the Underground Man, Dostoyevsky emphasizes all humans are flawed and warns against the dangers of idealistic thinking." The author will argue that through the Underground Man, Dostoyevsky sends a message about human nature.

Argument One

The author's first argument states: "To point out his views against idealistic principles, Dostoyevsky creates an antihero who attempts to live out these principles and fails." In this section, the author states the Underground Man mirrors socialists and fails as a result.

Man argues people care too much about their own status and interests to be able to form a perfect society. Through the defiantly antiheroic character of the Underground Man, Dostoyevsky emphasizes all humans are flawed and warns against the dangers of idealistic thinking.

To point out his views against idealistic principles, Dostoyevsky creates an antihero who attempts to live out these principles and fails. The Underground Man is a parody of intellectuals who mistakenly applies high ideals to a complex world. Specifically, Dostoyevsky aims at radical Russian intellectuals of the 1860s who sought to create a socialist society as the answer to Russia's problems. These intellectuals believed if people were enlightened, they would naturally do what was best for society. Therefore, by educating people about the right way to think, these intellectuals could eradicate many social problems, such as inequality and immorality, and create an ideal society. Dostoyevsky believed this was unrealistic because people are flawed. He thought any attempt to make them conform to high ideals was bound to fail.

The Underground Man is actually an indecisive intellectual, but he dreams of being a heroic man of action, someone who can act decisively and with certainty he is right. He enters the bar with the intention of getting into a fight. Instead, he ends up humiliated when an officer simply picks him up and moves him aside. He is too small and weak to actually be taken seriously in a fight, but he does not give up and accept it. Instead, he obsesses over the incident for years. He considers whether he can earn the bully's respect

Argument Two

Argument two speaks further to Dostoyevsky's view that humans are flawed: "The Underground Man is actually an indecisive intellectual, but he dreams of being a heroic man of action, someone who can act decisively and with certainty he is right."

and friendship by writing a beautiful letter, or humiliate him with a satirical story but, of course, he is delusional to think either of these will have an effect over brute strength. His final revenge—a tiny bump he feels more than the lieutenant does—illustrates the pathetic attempt to pit an intellectual against a soldier.

Argument Three

The third argument states: "The Underground Man attempts to use his high ideals to impress his peers but fails miserably." The author will present ways in which the Underground Man humiliates himself while trying to impress his peers with high ideals.

The Underground Man attempts to use his high ideals to impress his peers but fails miserably. Unlike Zverkov, who wins his friends' respect through his easy charm, good looks, and money, the Underground Man is not socially successful. He is unpleasant, unsociable, unsuccessful, and unattractive. He cannot relate to people, and people do not seem to like or admire him. Bitter about his lack of popularity, he tries impressing his friends with his superior intellect and his idealistic notions. But these are only empty ideals to him, and he realizes as he says them that his words are meaningless. People will always admire those who are wealthy, successful, good looking, and charming. He knows preaching to them about higher ideals will never change this fact.

Unable to influence his friends, the Underground Man attempts to become a social reformer. The narrator parodies the attempts of intellectuals who believe they can eradicate social ills, such as prostitution, simply by enlightening people about moral principles. He attempts to reform Liza, a prostitute, by lecturing her about her life. He gives an impassioned speech about the wonders of marriage and motherhood, hoping to motivate her through these high principles. But instead she's skeptical, telling him his words sound as if they come out of a book. Again, the narrator repeats empty ideals he himself does not believe. He is a hypocrite, only lecturing Liza to help make himself feel better and not out of any real desire to improve her life.

Ultimately, the Underground Man's failure to become a hero is his overly rigid adherence to the standards he has read about in books, which have no

Argument Four

In the fourth argument, the author presents the Underground Man as a social reformist who still fails in his pursuit: "Unable to influence his friends, the Underground Man attempts to become a social reformer."

Argument Five

In the author's final
argument, she highlights
the main character's
ultimate failure to be a hero:
"Ultimately, the Underground
Man's failure to become
a hero is his overly rigid
adherence to the standards
he has read about in books,
which have no application in
the real world."

application in the real world. When Liza shows up unexpectedly at his house, in a true state of need, he is mortified she will see he is really no role model but a pathetic man with a raggedy bathrobe who bullies his own servant. "They won't let me . . . I can't be . . . good!"[2] he finally exclaims to Liza in despair at not being able to live up to the standard of the rescuing hero. Filled with shame, he sends her out of his house, only to realize too late he has lost his one opportunity for true love.

He thinks he can achieve honor through a fight, but he cannot pit his intellect against brute strength. He thinks he can win his peers' admiration through spouting empty ideals, but he cannot win their respect without befriending them. He thinks he can effect social change by moralizing, but what he really needs to do is show love and acceptance. Having discovered he is no hero, the Underground Man refuses also to be a follower, or insect. By "insect," he means a useful member of a collective society who works, antlike,

A statue of Dostoyevsky stands in his honor in Omsk, Russia.

steadily toward a goal. If he could only be an insect,
he might have something to offer society. Failing in
either role, he concludes he has not been able to become

anything in his life, "neither wicked nor good, neither a scoundrel nor an honest man, neither a hero nor an insect."[3]

In reality, the Underground Man is simply human. Although the narrator seems to present a negative view of human nature, he actually celebrates human beings for all their faults and champions their right to free will and individuality. The Underground Man is a pathetic and sometimes despicable antihero, yet he stands defiantly as an example of why one cannot change the world armed only with high ideals and empty words. Through *Notes from the Underground*, Dostoyevsky argues leaders who try to control others or dictate morals to them will ultimately fail because people are complex and unpredictable, with whims and motives that do not make logical sense. Any attempt to mold people into heroic leaders or dutiful insects would result in a dangerous threat to their humanity.

Conclusion

The final paragraph concludes the author's critique and summarizes the thesis, stating the Underground Man is an antihero who proves one single person cannot reform society.

Thinking Critically

Now it's your turn to assess the critique. Consider these questions:

1. The thesis of this essay claims the Underground Man represents a realistic view of human nature and champions free will. Do you agree with this? Why or why not?

2. What additional points or anecdotes from the book could have helped support the thesis?

3. The conclusion should restate the thesis and the main arguments of the essay. Does this conclusion do so effectively? Explain.

Other Approaches

You have just read an analysis of Dostoyevsky's *Notes from the Underground* that discusses the political climate of the times in which Dostoyevsky wrote. Consider other approaches you could take to the work. One approach could be biographical, looking into the author's own biases and opinions and how those reflect on a work. Another approach could contrast two of the book's characters.

Biographical Criticism

Biographical criticism seeks to relate a literary work to the author's own life. A possible thesis for an essay that examines *Notes from the Underground* from a biographical perspective might be: Dostoyevsky makes it clear the Underground Man is a fictional character and does not necessarily represent himself or his own views.

Compare and Contrast

Another way to approach the antihero in *Notes from the Underground* might be to compare the Underground Man with the character of Zverkov. Why is Zverkov successful and popular whereas the Underground Man is not, and what does that say about society and people's values? A possible thesis statement that views the antihero in this way might be: The Underground Man is the antihero, overly conscious and paralyzed by self-doubt, whereas Zverkov represents the hero because he is confident and active.

8

AN OVERVIEW OF
Native Son

*R*ichard Wright's novel *Native Son* was published in 1940. It tells the story of Bigger Thomas, a young black man living in poverty on the south side of Chicago, Illinois, in the 1930s. In writing *Native Son,* Wright intended to present the ugly truth about racism in the United States as he had seen and lived it. Wright himself was an African-American writer who grew up in the segregated South. In the South, laws kept blacks separate from whites in all areas of life. Blacks were not allowed to eat in the same restaurants, attend the same schools, or sit in the same train cars as white people. They were raised to fear whites. If they dared offend a white person, they could be charged with a crime.

As an adult, Wright moved to Chicago. He was one of thousands of southern African Americans who moved

Richard Wright wrote about segregation and racial oppression
after experiencing it firsthand.

to the North in search of a better life during what is known as the Great Migration (1910–1930). However, life in the North proved even worse in some ways than life in the South. Poor urban blacks lived in crowded ghettoes. White landlords would not rent to them in white neighborhoods, and racism kept them out of many jobs and schools. The situation grew even worse during the Great Depression of the 1930s, the time in which this book is set. In *Native Son,* Wright gives a realistic picture of this oppressive environment and how it affected African Americans.

Book 1: Fear

The first part of the novel is entitled "Fear," as it details the life of fear and anger Bigger Thomas inhabits. As book 1 opens, Bigger Thomas wakes up in his family's tiny one-room apartment to the sound of an alarm clock. Bigger, his younger brother, Buddy, his sister, Vera, and his mother turn their backs to avoid seeing one another get dressed. A huge black rat runs out, terrifying the women. While Buddy blocks the entrance to the rat's hole, Bigger chases the rat and kills it with a cooking skillet.

Native Son was made into a 1951 film.

Bigger dangles the dead rat in his sister's face, taunting her until she faints with fear. His mother scolds him for scaring his sister and for not caring enough to support the family. She warns prophetically that if he does not straighten out, he will end up dead. Bigger shuts her voice out of his mind. He hates his family because he feels powerless to ease their suffering.

As he prepares to leave, his mother reminds Bigger if he does not take the job the government relief agency is offering, their food supply will be cut off. He shouts that he will take it and then slams the door. On the street, Bigger thinks about how he is sick of his life and about his lack of choices. He can take the relief job, offered by a man named Mr. Dalton, or starve. He looks up and sees a large signboard depicting the public figure Buckley, a corrupt state's attorney. The figure of Buckley is pointing his finger straight out at the street. Above him are the words "YOU CAN'T WIN!"[1]

Attempting Change

Bigger meets his friend Gus at a poolroom. The two joke about white people. Bigger confesses to Gus that thinking of white people gives him a pain. He fears something awful is going to happen or he is going to do something he cannot help. Joined by their friends G. H. and Jack, they discuss their plan to rob a white-owned deli. This would be the first time any of them has robbed a white man, and they are all afraid, but none of them wants to admit it.

Before the robbery, Bigger and Jack go to the movies. A newsreel before the feature shows a white socialite on a beach in Florida. It is Mary Dalton, the daughter of the man who offered Bigger a job. Bigger is fascinated by the picture of white wealth and decides he wants the job. Back at the poolroom, Bigger wants to back out of the robbery. Rather than admit he is afraid to rob a white man, Bigger picks a fight with Gus, threatening to slit his throat with a knife. The friends call off the robbery.

The next day, Bigger meets Henry Dalton, who offers him a job as chauffeur. Dalton is a millionaire who owns much of the real estate on Chicago's south side. He charges black people high rent and will not let them rent in other areas of the city. At the same time, he and his wife, Mrs. Dalton, are philanthropists who support black organizations. They want to hire Bigger to give him an opportunity. Bigger is awed by the Daltons' mansion, where for the first time he will have his very own room. The Daltons' maid, Peggy, warns him to watch out for Mary Dalton, who she says is a wild girl.

That evening, Bigger drives Mary, who is a college student, to a meeting at the university. But instead of going to school, she directs Bigger to take her to see her boyfriend, Jan Erlone. Her parents do not approve of Jan because he is a communist who believes in overthrowing the rich and sharing the wealth and property equally among people. Jan tells Bigger there will be a revolution,

Bigger takes the job as Mr. Dalton's chauffeur, driving Mary and Jan.

and after that "things'll be different. There'll be no white and no black; there'll be no rich and no poor."[2] Jan and Mary attempt to befriend Bigger by sitting next to him in the car and inviting him to eat with them, but Bigger, who has learned he must keep his distance from white people, is bewildered and afraid. He feels humiliated when Mary asks him about his life because she wants to know how black people live.

At dinner, Jan and Mary buy a bottle of rum. They get drunk and kiss in the car. Jan leaves and has Bigger drive Mary home. She is so drunk she leans on Bigger and asks him to carry her up to her room, and she allows him to kiss her. Just then, Mrs. Dalton opens the door looking for Mary. She is blind and cannot see Bigger, but Bigger panics, thinking she will find out he is in the bedroom with Mary and he will be accused of rape. He covers Mary's mouth with a pillow to stop her from saying anything in her drunken state. Mrs. Dalton smells alcohol and scolds Mary for being drunk then leaves the room. Bigger removes the pillow and realizes he has accidentally suffocated Mary to death.

Panicked, Bigger decides to hide his crime by burning Mary's body in the furnace. He has to cut off her head to make her fit inside. Then he adds more coal to the fire. He decides to tell the Daltons Jan was the one who took Mary up to her room that night, and when they find she is missing, they will think she has run off with Jan and the communists.

Book 2: Flight

In the second section, Bigger attempts to flee his crime. But he feels a strange sense of empowerment after killing Mary. He visits his girlfriend Bessie and gives her a wad of money he has stolen from Mary's room and tells her he plans to hold Mary for ransom. Bessie will be the one to collect the money. Bessie, a downtrodden young woman who works for a white family all week and then escapes through alcohol, agrees with his plan, even though she is afraid Bigger has done something to Mary.

Dalton hires a private detective, Mr. Britten, to find out what has happened to his daughter. Bigger purposely plays the part of a simple black boy and manipulates them into suspecting Jan has caused Mary's disappearance. Meanwhile, Bigger writes a false ransom note demanding money for Mary's safe return. He sees this as a way of getting back at Mr. Dalton as a slumlord who profits from blacks. The Daltons contact the police, who continue to suspect Mary's communist friends. News reporters visit the house and get a statement from Mr. Dalton saying he will pay the ransom. While the reporters are gathered, the furnace begins smoking badly. One of the reporters tries to help Bigger clean out the ashes, and Mary's bones are discovered in the furnace.

Amid the confusion, Bigger escapes by jumping out of a window into the snow. He goes to Bessie and tells

Bigger, who is played by Richard Wright himself in the 1951 film, at first confides in Bessie.

her what happened. Bessie is terrified and cries bitterly, regretting she ever knew Bigger. He drags her off with him to an abandoned building to hide for the night. He rapes Bessie, and while she is sleeping, he decides he has no choice but to kill her. Running with her will only slow him down, and he cannot leave her behind because she knows too much. He murders Bessie by smashing in her head with a brick. He then throws her body down an air shaft, after which he realizes she has all his money in her pocket. Afraid to go down and retrieve the money, Bigger flees, penniless.

Bigger runs through the city and hides in vacant apartments. Along the way, he hears people talking and finds out the police are searching Chicago, looking for him. The police eventually corner him on a rooftop and he is taken into custody.

Book 3: Fate

Book 3 begins with Bigger in jail, fulfilling the fate that was waiting for him all along. He refuses to eat or drink. Jan visits him, and Bigger is surprised Jan treats him like a human being. For the first time, he actually sees a white person as human. He experiences remorse for what he has done to hurt Jan.

Jan helps Bigger hire a communist lawyer named Max. As Bigger talks to Max, he comes to understand himself and his actions. For the first time in his life, he feels connected to others and wants to live. But it is too late. He stands to get the death penalty for murder. A mob gathers, calling for him to be lynched. The state's attorney, Buckley, gets him to confess to the murders and pressures him to admit to many other murders as well as the rape of Mary Dalton. Bigger vehemently denies he raped Mary or killed other women. In court, however, Buckley repeats racist stereotypes by arguing Bigger is a "black ape" motivated by a desire to rape and kill.[3] Max, on the other hand, eloquently describes Bigger's disadvantaged life. He argues Bigger is a social symbol, a powerless pawn in a racist society, who did what he did because he thought he had no other choice. Bigger is sentenced to death, but Max's speech indicates Bigger's execution will not solve the larger problem: the societal sickness of inequality. This sickness, he says, has created a dangerous force in US society, a revolutionary force that "has sharpened its claws."[4]

9

Antihero as Social Protest

Similar to many black writers of his time, Wright used fiction as a tool to protest racial inequality. Wright, however, believed other black writers had been too sentimental. They had attempted to appeal to white people's pity by writing books about good and noble African Americans, heroes who struggled and suffered. Bigger Thomas, the central character in Wright's 1940 novel, *Native Son,* is the opposite of a likeable hero. A bully, thug, and murderer who takes pride in his crimes, he seems more like a monster. Wright does not expect readers to pity Bigger or empathize with him. Instead, he wants readers to interpret Bigger as a product of a racist society, destined from birth to become exactly who he is. In creating the character of Bigger, a black,

In *Native Son*, Bigger Thomas becomes an antihero readers sympathize with.

Thesis Statement

The thesis of the essay appears at the end of the first paragraph: "In creating the character of Bigger, a black, murderous antihero, Wright shows the dark side of racism—the hatred and fear constant oppression breeds in a person's mind and the resulting violence." In this essay, the author will argue that Wright purposely made the character Bigger an antihero to highlight the negative effect his racist society has on him.

Argument One

The first argument states: "Oppressed by a racist society, Bigger is powerless and trapped." Bigger is led to crime because he feels powerless and is unable to move up in society because of his race.

murderous antihero, Wright shows the dark side of racism—the hatred and fear constant oppression breeds in a person's mind and the resulting violence.

Oppressed by a racist society, Bigger is powerless and trapped. Bigger's neighborhood is a black ghetto on the south side of Chicago, where blacks are "bottled up . . . like wild animals" because white landlords will not rent to them in any other neighborhood.[1] Bigger lives in a rat-infested one-room apartment with his mother, sister, and brother. Since his father was killed in racial violence in the South, his mother looks to Bigger to support the family. In 1930s Chicago, racism meant employment opportunities were limited for a black man. As he describes it to Max: "You get a little job here and a little job there. You shine shoes, sweep streets; anything. . . . You don't make enough to live on. You don't know when you going to get fired. Pretty soon you get so you can't hope for nothing."[2]

Bigger once had dreams of becoming an aviator, but he learned nonwhite students were not allowed to attend flight school. The military does not offer blacks any real opportunities, either: "All they want a black man for is to dig ditches . . . wash dishes and scrub floors."[3] When Bigger steps out onto the street with his friend Gus, he sees a political sign reading "YOU CAN'T WIN." These words might well be directed to him and all other blacks. Bigger knows he cannot win in a white man's world, and it enrages him.

Bigger's lack of power fills him with rage, fear, and hatred, which he takes out on his family and community. He bullies his sister, curses his mother, and robs black businesses. He attacks and humiliates his

Argument Two

Next, the author explains how racism has affected Bigger's mind, making him lash out in anger: "Bigger's lack of power fills him with rage, fear, and hatred, which he takes out on his family and community."

friend Gus because he is ashamed to admit he is afraid of robbing a white man. As he looks back on it later, he realizes he was consumed with a "deep, choking hate . . . a hate that he had not wanted to have, but could not help having."[4] Above all, he hates and fears white people, as they hate and fear him. It is Bigger's fear of white people that leads him to kill Mary Dalton, as he finds himself caught in her bedroom in a position where he might be accused of rape.

Argument Three

The third argument explains how Mary's death is the result of white people's misunderstandings of racism: "Racism has warped Bigger's view of white people so much he feels a sense of empowerment instead of remorse after killing Mary Dalton, showcasing his antiheroic personality."

Racism has warped Bigger's view of white people so much he feels a sense of empowerment instead of remorse after killing Mary Dalton, showcasing his antiheroic personality. Because she is white, Mary was never a real person to Bigger. Strangely, he feels excited, as if in committing murder he is creating a new life for himself, getting back at white people who laughed at him for being "black and clownlike."[5] Later, he realizes "the knowledge that he had killed a white girl they loved and regarded

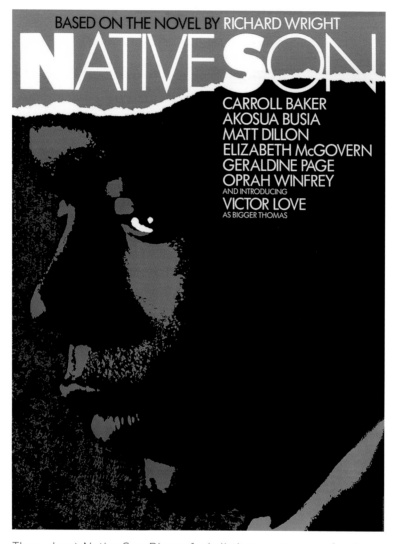

BASED ON THE NOVEL BY RICHARD WRIGHT

NATIVE SON

CARROLL BAKER
AKOSUA BUSIA
MATT DILLON
ELIZABETH McGOVERN
GERALDINE PAGE
OPRAH WINFREY
AND INTRODUCING
VICTOR LOVE
AS BIGGER THOMAS

Throughout *Native Son*, Bigger feels little to no remorse for the actions his society drives him to.

as their symbol of beauty made him feel the equal of them, like a man who had been somehow cheated, but had now evened the score."[6] Even at the end of the book, Bigger confesses, "I ain't worried none about them women I killed. For a little while I was free. I was doing something. It was wrong, but I was feeling all right. . . . I wasn't scared no more for a little while."[7] His lack of guilt highlights his antiheroic characteristics and opinions.

In covering up the crime, Bigger continues to feel empowered. He uses the white detectives' racist assumptions and prejudices against communists to turn suspicion away from himself and onto Jan over Mary's disappearance. He reasons: "In the past had they not always drawn the picture for him? He could tell them anything he wanted and what could they do about it? It was his word against Jan's."[8] Bigger decides to send the ransom note after he reflects on Mr. Dalton's position as an oppressor: "Even though Mr. Dalton gave millions of dollars for Negro education, he would rent houses to Negroes only in this prescribed area, this corner of the city tumbling down from rot."[9] Even after killing Bessie, he retains a "sense of power. *He* had done this. *He* had brought all this about. In all of his life these two murders were the most meaningful things that had ever happened to him. He was living, truly and deeply, no matter what others might think."[10]

Ultimately, Bigger realizes he is not in control of his own destiny and is instead a powerless pawn of social forces beyond his understanding. Bigger is captured, jailed, and sentenced to death—the fate society had in mind for someone like him all along. He is not surprised: "I knew at some time or other they was going to get me for something. I'm black."[11] A mob cries for Bigger to be lynched. In his argument before the court, Buckley depicts Bigger as a "black mad dog" whose actions were motivated by lust, greed, and the desire to kill—the racist stereotype of an African-American criminal.[12] But readers know this is a false picture. Neither Bigger nor his lawyer, Max, claim Bigger is innocent of the crimes. He is guilty. But as Max puts it, life in a racist society left Bigger "hemmed in, limited, circumscribed" so he saw and felt "no way of acting except to hate and kill that which he thinks is crushing him."[13] Through Max's speech, Wright does not mean to excuse Bigger for his horrible crimes, but

In the final argument, the author explains why, although Bigger is guilty, he is in a larger sense not to blame for his crimes: "Ultimately, Bigger realizes he is not in control of his own destiny and is instead a powerless pawn of social forces beyond his understanding."

As he is arrested and says goodbye to his mother, Bigger realizes he cannot escape his fate.

shows he is an antihero, shaped by his environment. A society sick with racism breeds sick people. Bigger should not be viewed as only a common criminal but a figure of social protest—one among millions of others, black and white, who will inevitably strike out violently in response to an unjust system.

Thinking Critically

Now it's your turn to assess the critique. Consider these questions:

1. After reading the essay, do you think the author did a good job proving the thesis? Why or why not?

2. What was the most interesting argument made? What was the strongest one? What was the weakest? Were the points backed up with examples from the novel? Did the argument support the thesis?

3. Read the novel for yourself. Do you agree Bigger Thomas is a powerless pawn in a racist society? What do you believe about him?

Other Approaches

What you have just read is one examination of the antihero in *Native Son*. Can you think of other ways to approach this topic? Another way to study *Native Son* is through Marxist criticism, analyzing the ways in which Marxist theory shines through in the novel. Biographical criticism could also be applied to *Native Son*, examining the ways in which Wright's own life experiences are reflected in the work.

Marxist Criticism

Marxist criticism involves examining a work in relation to the ideas of German philosopher Karl Marx. Marx believed society could not be healthy until power and wealth were shared equally by all. At the time he wrote this novel, Richard Wright was a member of the Communist Party, a political group aimed at applying Marx's ideas to government. A thesis statement reflecting a Marxist criticism of *Native Son* might read: In *Native Son*, author Richard Wright convincingly shows communism is a solution to social ills.

Biographical Criticism

Biographical criticism aims to examine a work in relation to the author's life. You have read that Richard Wright was a member of the Communist Party. It is possible many of the author's same ideas and beliefs about society are reflected in *Native Son*. A thesis statement that argues Richard Wright's biographical information correlates to his novel might read: In *Native Son*, author Richard Wright conveys his own favoring thoughts about communism by contrasting the antiheroic character Bigger Thomas against compassionate, communist Jan.

Analyze It!

Now that you have examined the theme of the antihero, are you ready to perform your own analysis? You have read that this type of evaluation can help you look at literature in a new way and make you pay attention to certain issues you may not have otherwise recognized. So, why not look for an antihero theme in one or more of your favorite books?

First, choose the work you want to analyze. Who is the main character? Is he or she an antihero? How so? Does the antihero grow or change? If you choose to compare the theme in more than one work, what do they have in common? How do they differ? Next, write a specific question about the theme that interests you. Then you can form your thesis, which should provide the answer to that question. Your thesis is the most important part of your analysis and offers an argument about the work, considering the theme, its effect on the characters, or what it says about society or the world. Recall that the thesis statement typically appears at the very end of the introductory paragraph of your essay. It is usually only one sentence long.

After you have written your thesis, find evidence to back it up. Good places to start are in the work itself or in journals or articles that discuss what other people have said about it. You may also want to read about the author or creator's life so you can get a sense of what factors may have affected the creative process. This can be especially useful if you are considering how the theme connects to history or the author's intent.

You should also explore parts of the book that seem to disprove your thesis and create an argument against them. As you do this, you might want to address what others have written about the book. Their quotes may help support your claim.

Before you start analyzing a work, think about the different arguments made in this book. Reflect on how evidence supporting the thesis was presented. Did you find that some of the techniques used to back up the arguments were more convincing than others? Try these methods as you prove your thesis in your own critique.

When you are finished writing your critique, read it over carefully. Is your thesis statement understandable? Do the supporting arguments flow logically, with the topic of each paragraph clearly stated? Can you add any information that would present your readers with a stronger argument in favor of your thesis? Were you able to use quotes from the book, as well as from other critics, to enhance your ideas? Did you see the work in a new light?

Glossary

communism
A system of government in which all property is publically owned.

hero
A character in literature who represents the ideals of society, such as bravery and courage.

lynch
To kill someone illegally as punishment for a crime.

moor
An open, rocky landscape with fiercely blowing winds.

parody
A piece of writing that imitates another work with the purpose of mocking or poking fun at the original author's message.

patriarchal
Male-dominated.

philanthropist
Someone of wealth who donates money and time to improve the lives of others.

racism
Poor treatment of or violence against people because of their race.

satire
A literary technique that uses humor to show someone or something is foolish.

sexton
A church officer who takes care of the church property.

socialism
A political and economic theory that advocates resources and property being shared equally among members of society.

soliloquy
In drama, a speech delivered by a character who is alone onstage.

stereotype
An often unfair and untrue belief that many people have about all people or things with a particular characteristic—for example, gender or race.

thane
A Scottish nobleman who owns land and is obligated to perform service to his king.

tragedy
A drama, or play, that depicts a hero of high status whose foolish or evil actions lead to a tragic downfall.

tragic hero
The hero of a tragedy. The tragic hero experiences a downfall as a result of a tragic flaw, typically pride or ambition.

wuther
To blow with a dull roaring sound.

Characteristics
AND CLASSICS

The antihero is a common theme in literature. Antiheroic characters in literature, art, and film starkly oppose the hero archetype. Antiheroes may be villainous, lack courage, or break the rules to get ahead.

This theme often includes:

- A main or secondary character who serves as the work's antihero
- A call to action or journey the antihero must fight for or against
- Protagonists the antihero must confront
- Challenges or obstacles the antihero must overcome

Some famous works with an antihero theme are:

- Alexandre Dumas and Auguste Maquet's *The Count of Monte Cristo*
- F. Scott Fitzgerald's *The Great Gatsby*
- Margaret Mitchell's *Gone with the Wind*
- J. D. Salinger's *The Catcher in the Rye*
- Chuck Palahniuk's *Fight Club*
- Gillian Flynn's *Gone Girl*

References

Brontë, Emily. *Wuthering Heights.* New York: Knopf, 1991. Print.

Butler, Robert. *Native Son: The Emergence of a New Black Hero.*
Boston: Twayne, 1991. Print.

Dostoyevsky, Fyodor. *Notes from the Underground.* Trans. by Richard
Pevear and Larissa Volokhonsky. New York: Knopf, 1993. Print.

Oates, Joyce Carol. "The Magnanimity of *Wuthering Heights.*"
Celestial Timepiece. Celestial Timepiece, 27 Jan. 2015. Web.
2 Feb. 2015.

Reed, Walter. *Meditations on the Hero: A Study of the Romantic Hero in
Nineteenth-Century Fiction.* New Haven: Yale UP, 1974. Print.

Shakespeare, William. *The Tragedy of Macbeth.* Ed. Barbara A. Mowat
and Paul Werstine, Folger Shakespeare Library. New York:
Simon, 2013. Print.

Thorslev, Peter L., Jr. *The Byronic Hero: Types and Prototypes.*
Minneapolis: U of Minnesota, 1965. Print.

Wright, Richard. *Native Son.* 1940. New York: Harper, 2005. Print.

Additional
RESOURCES

Further Readings

Simmons, David. *The Anti-Hero in the American Novel: From Heller to Vonnegut.* New York: Palgrave Macmillan, 2008. Print.

Stein, Atara. *The Byronic Hero in Film, Fiction and Television.* Carbondale: Southern Illinois UP, 2009. Print.

Wright, Richard. *Black Boy.* New York: Harper, 2007. Print.

Websites

To learn more about Essential Literary Themes, visit **booklinks.abdopublishing.com**. These links are routinely monitored and updated to provide the most current information available.

Places to Visit

The Brontë Society and Brontë Parsonage Museum
Church Street, Haworth
West Yorkshire, UK BD228DR
http://www.bronte.org.uk
Visit the home of authors Emily, Charlotte, and Anne Brontë and their family in Yorkshire, United Kingdom. Or, if you cannot make the trip, visit the website or write the Brontë society for more information about the Brontë sisters and their legacies.

The Folger Shakespeare Library
201 E. Capitol St. SE
Washington, DC 20003
http://www.folger.edu
The Folger Shakespeare Library, located in Washington, DC, is the world's largest collection of Shakespeare materials. The library maintains a digital collection of Shakespeare's plays.

F. M. Dostoyevsky Literary-Memorial Museum
191002 Saint Petersburg, Kuznechny Lane, 5/2
Russia
http://eng.md.spb.ru/museum
Fyodor Dostoyevsky's former home in Saint Petersburg is maintained as a museum. Visit the museum's website to learn more about the Russian author's life and works.

Source Notes

Chapter 1. Introduction to Themes in Literature
None.

Chapter 2. An Overview of *Macbeth*
1. William Shakespeare. *The Tragedy of Macbeth*. Ed. Barbara A. Mowat and Paul Werstine, Folger Shakespeare Library. New York: Simon, 2013. Print. 29.
2. Ibid. 31.
3. Ibid. 33.
4. Ibid. 125.
5. Ibid. 127.
6. Ibid. 177.
7. Ibid.
8. Ibid. 125.

Chapter 3. Feminist Antihero
1. William Shakespeare. *The Tragedy of Macbeth*. Ed. Barbara A. Mowat and Paul Werstine, Folger Shakespeare Library. New York: Simon, 2013. Print. 31.
2. Ibid.
3. Ibid. 33.
4. Ibid. 103.

Chapter 4. An Overview of *Wuthering Heights*
1. Emily Brontë. *Wuthering Heights*. New York: Knopf, 1991. Print. 31.
2. Ibid. 56.
3. Ibid. 191.
4. Ibid. 385.

Chapter 5. Romantic Antihero
1. Emily Brontë. *Wuthering Heights*. New York: Knopf, 1991. Print. 1.
2. Ibid. 64.
3. Ibid. 109.
4. Ibid. 4.
5. Ibid. 65.
6. Ibid. 65.
7. Ibid. 314.
8. Ibid. 174.
9. Ibid. 172.
10. Joyce Carol Oates. "The Magnanimity of *Wuthering Heights*." *Celestial Timepiece*. Celestial Timepiece, 27 Jan. 2015. Web. 2 Feb. 2015.
11. Emily Brontë. *Wuthering Heights*. New York: Knopf, 1991. Print. 116.

Chapter 6. An Overview of *Notes from the Underground*

1. Fyodor Dostoyevsky. *Notes from the Underground*. Trans. By Richard Pevear and Larissa Volokhonsky. New York: Knopf, 1993. Print. 7.
2. Ibid. 41.
3. Ibid. 43.
4. Ibid. 72.

Chapter 7. Alienated Antihero

1. Fyodor Dostoyevsky. *Notes from the Underground*. Trans. By Richard Pevear and Larissa Volokhonsky. New York: Knopf, 1993. Print. 36.
2. Ibid. 113.
3. Ibid. 7.

Chapter 8. An Overview of *Native Son*

1. Richard Wright. *Native Son*. New York: Harper, 2005. Print. 13.
2. Ibid. 68.
3. Ibid. 408.
4. Ibid. 392.

Chapter 9. Antihero as Social Protest

1. Richard Wright. *Native Son*. New York: Harper, 2005. Print. 249.
2. Ibid. 353.
3. Ibid. 353.
4. Ibid. 308.
5. Ibid. 150.
6. Ibid. 164.
7. Ibid. 354.
8. Ibid. 158.
9. Ibid. 174.
10. Ibid. 239.
11. Ibid. 351.
12. Ibid. 409.
13. Ibid. 390.

Index

abuse, 36, 37, 48, 40, 91–92
alienated antihero, 11, 64–72
Apollon, 63
archetypes, 7, 30, 31

Banquo, 14, 18–19, 20
Bessie, 84–86, 94
Britten, Mr., 84
Brontë, Anne, 32
Brontë, Charlotte, 32
Brontë, Emily, 32–34, 42, 44, 48,
  49, 50, 53
Buckley, 80, 87, 95
Buddy, 78, 90
Byron, George Gordon, 34
Byronic hero, 34, 44

communism, 56, 81, 83, 84, 87, 94,
  98, 99

Dalton, Henry, 80, 81, 83, 84, 94
Dalton, Mary, 80, 81–84, 87, 92, 94
Dalton, Mrs., 81, 83, 84
Dean, Ellen "Nelly," 37, 39, 40, 45,
  47
Dostoyevsky, Fyodor, 54–56,
  64–67, 72, 74
Duncan, 14–16, 17, 18, 19, 26

Earnshaw, Cathy, 32, 38–41, 42,
  46–50, 52
Earnshaw, Hareton, 40
Earnshaw, Mr., 37–38
Erlone, Jan, 81–82, 83, 84, 86–87,
  94, 99

feminist antihero, 22–28, 52
Ferfichkin, 60
Fleance, 19

G. H., 80
Gothic fiction, 32
Gothic villain, 44
Great Depression, 78
Great Migration, 78
guilt, 17, 20, 26, 94, 95
Gus, 80, 81, 91, 92

Heathcliff, 32–41, 42–50, 51, 52, 53
Hindley, 36, 37–38, 39, 40, 47
humiliation, 39, 60, 61, 63, 67, 68,
  82, 91

Jack, 80

Lady Macbeth, 12, 15–21, 22–28,
  29, 30, 31
Lennox, 18, 19
Linton, Catherine, 35, 37, 40, 41,
  48, 52
Linton, Edgar, 38, 39–40, 41, 52
Linton, Isabella, 38, 40–41, 48
Liza, 62–63, 69–70
Lockwood, Mr., 34–37, 41, 45–46

Macbeth, 12–21, 22–28, 29, 30, 31
Macbeth, 12–21, 24, 25, 26, 30, 31
Macduff, 18, 19, 20, 21
Malcolm, 14–15, 18, 20–21
marriage, 24, 25, 39, 41, 48, 52,
  62, 69
Marx, Karl, 54, 98
Max, 87, 91, 95
mockery, 40, 49, 56, 61
murder, 12, 15, 16, 18, 20, 26, 30,
  86, 87, 88, 90, 92, 94

Native Son, 76–87, 88–96, 97, 98, 99
Nicholas I, 56
nihilists, 56
Notes from the Underground, 54–63, 64–72, 73, 74, 75

Oates, Joyce Carol, 49
oppression, 54, 78, 90, 94

Peggy, 81
predictions, 14–15, 18, 20, 21

racism, 76, 78, 90, 91, 92, 96
reade-response criticism, 42, 52
remorse, 26, 28, 86, 92
romantic hero, 40, 44, 46–47, 48
Romeo and Juliet, 12, 47

segregation, 76
Shakespeare, William, 12, 22, 24, 26–28, 30, 47
Simonov, 60, 62
social protest, 88–96
social reform, 56, 69
society, 8, 11, 22, 24, 28, 29, 52, 54, 56, 57, 64–67, 70–71, 72, 75, 87, 88, 90, 95, 96, 97, 98, 99
stereotypes, 25, 49, 87, 95
sympathy, 11, 22, 46, 53

Thomas, Bigger, 76–87, 88–96, 97, 99
Thrushcross Grange, 34–35, 37, 38, 40, 41
tragic flaw, 12
Trudolyubov, 60

Underground Man, 57–63, 64–72, 73, 74, 75
utilitarianism, 64

Vera, 78–79, 90, 91

witches, 14–15, 18, 20–21, 30
Wright, Richard, 76–78, 88–90, 95, 96, 98, 99
Wuthering Heights, 32–41, 42–50, 51, 52, 53
Wuthering Heights, 35, 37, 39, 40, 47

Zverkov, 60–61, 68, 75

About the Author

Jennifer Joline Anderson lives in Minneapolis, Minnesota, where she writes educational books for young people. She has written many books for Abdo Publishing, including *Great American Authors: Langston Hughes* and *Essential Library of Social Change: Women's Rights Movement*.